ERNST HAAS

ERNST

HAAS

Bryn
Campbell

COLLINS

ERNST HAAS

by Bryn Campbell

Ernst Haas, photographed by Richard Rowan

'No photographer has worked more successfully to express the sheer physical joy of seeing.' This is how, in 1962, John Szarkowski, Director of the Department of Photography at the Museum of Modern Art, New York, described the achievement of Ernst Haas. It was a deserved tribute and one that only a colour photographer could wholly merit. Whatever the special qualities and pleasures of the black and white medium, only colour can do justice to the full sensuous richness of vision.

Haas has specialized in colour for over 20 years and he finds it personally more demanding than monochrome. 'I think the challenge is so much greater in colour. In black and white you only have grey tones. In colour you have the most incredible combinations of subtle tints which you can use for depths or for accents. Black and white is a wonderful medium for getting to the human essentials as fast as possible. For instance, if you are photographing a situation where the main subject is wearing grey but a secondary figure is in red, your eye will constantly be drawn towards the latter. Working in black and white there would be no real problem, but with colour you would have to manoeuvre very carefully. It is more difficult to shoot colour, you have to think and feel in a totally different way.'

This personal preference does not distort his judgement, or spoil his enjoyment, of photography as a whole. He wrote recently, 'I still don't understand all these problematic discussions about colour versus black and white. I love both, but they do speak a different language within the same frame. Both are fascinating.

'Colour does not mean black and white plus colour, nor is black and white just a picture without colour. Each needs a different awareness in seeing and, because of this, a different discipline. The decisive moments in black and white and in colour are not identical.' He continued, 'There are black and white snobs, as well as colour snobs. Because of their inability to use both well, they act on the defensive and create camps. We should never judge a photographer by what film he uses—only by how he uses it.'

In fact, Haas first made his name as a black and white photographer—there was scarcely a choice for the photojournalist in the years immediately after the Second World War—and one of the earliest, and continuing, influences on his work were the black and white pictures of Edward Weston, the renowned American photographer.

Born in Vienna in 1921, Haas's early ambitions were to be a painter or an explorer, but the war interrupted any career he may have planned. At first he was assigned to the German Air Force, building and maintaining airfields, then he left to study medicine for a couple of years until the end of the war. Suddenly Haas had the chance to print his late father's negatives and his interest in photography, which earlier his father had tried to encourage, was greatly stimulated. He enrolled at an art college and began to study photography but his darkroom technique was not up to scratch and he had to leave the course. Still enthusiastic, he continued to work on his own, using a Rolleiflex camera acquired in a barter deal for 9 kg (20 lb) of margarine given to him as a birthday present by his wealthy brother. He managed to sell a few pictures and also taught photography to American soldiers at classes organized by the Red Cross. In 1946 he visited Switzerland and showed his prints to Alfred Kubler, editor of the magazine *Du,* who then introduced him to the work of photographer Werner Bischof. Haas and Bischof became friends and they both operated through the same picture agency, Black Star.

The following year Haas's first exhibition, at the American Red Cross Headquarters in Vienna, attracted the attention of Warran Trabant, editor of *Heute*, an American magazine for Germans in the occupied territories. Haas began to work for the journal and often teamed up with their correspondent, Inge Morath—later to become famous as a photographer herself.

The first major turning point for Haas came in 1949. On assignment to do a fashion feature, he photographed returning Austrian prisoners-of-war. *Heute* used the story prominently, then *Life* published it and offered Haas a staff job. But instead, he accepted Robert Capa's invitation to join the recently established agency, Magnum, because it seemed to promise him more creative freedom. 1949 was also the year he began to work in colour. He has explained how the change came about quite naturally. 'I was longing for it, needed it; I was ready for it, and there was a film available to work with . . . Kodachrome 1, rated at 12 ASA.' (The ASA number indicates a film's relative sensitivity to light.)

He feels that he was psychologically prepared for this change. 'I will always remember the war years—all the war years, including at least five bitter postwar years—as the black and white years, or even better, the grey years. Somehow, maybe quite symbolically, I wanted to express that the world and life had changed—as if everything was suddenly newly painted. The grey times were over; as at the beginning of a new spring I wanted to celebrate in colour the new times, filled with new hopes.'

With comparable symbolism, his first major colour essay rejoiced in his new home town, New York City. He emigrated to the United States in 1951 and two years later *Life* published *Images of a Magic City*—a two-part essay running to 24 pages, the longest colour story that the magazine had ever carried. Indeed, from a creative standpoint, colour photography was still in its infancy at that time. The technical limitations of the first generally available processes had been a severe handicap to pioneers in the medium and it was not until the mid-to-late thirties that more practical materials were marketed. Then came the war, with all the disruption that entailed. So it is not altogether surprising that, as late as 1951, Alexander Liberman wrote in his foreword to *The Art and Technique of Color Photography*, 'This book comes out at the threshold of the color era.'

Haas was to prove a major influence on the period that followed. It was soon obvious that he had a particular flair for working in colour, with a taste for subtle effects rather than garish display. He was not inhibited by the slow film speed of Kodachrome—its relative lack of sensitivity to light—but enthusiastically explored the most difficult lighting conditions. It is interesting to notice how often, and how powerfully, he used the device of the silhouette to cope with the limitations of his film during those early years.

In order to record shadow detail in poor light, a slow shutter speed was necessary. That meant carrying a tripod or always having to find some suitable place to steady the camera. Neither method was very convenient if one wanted to wander around freely, as unencumbered as possible, ready to respond quickly to any picture-making opportunities. There was another problem. The emulsion could only handle limited subject contrast, that is, the difference in exposure required by highlight and shadow areas. When that difference was too great, correct exposure for the shadows resulted in a loss of highlight detail, and vice versa.

Whether by instinct or reason, Haas occasionally turned to the silhouette as a

'Colour does not mean black and white plus colour, nor is black and white just a picture without colour . . . The decisive moments in black and white and in colour are not identical.'

Haas's creative curiosity led him to develop a style of photographing movement that is now indelibly associated with his name. A simple description of it is 'motion blur'.

way round both these difficulties. He ignored shadow detail and concentrated instead on outlining exciting forms against a background of light colour. It was, for instance, the technique he used in Venice, profiling gondolas and gondoliers against a twilight sky (pages 8 and 9). Contrast was no longer a problem but an aesthetic strength, and since exposure was calculated only for the highlights, much faster shutter speeds could be selected. Similar methods produced a wide variety of results in his coverages of New York, London, France and Spain.

His creative curiosity also led him to develop a style of photographing movement that is now indelibly associated with his name. A simple description of it is 'motion blur'.

Instead of 'freezing' subject movement with a fast shutter speed, Haas used a slow speed so that the subject continued to move during exposure, thereby creating a blurred image. He learned how to control the nature and degree of that blur by the choice of shutter speed and movement of the camera in relation to the action of the subject. The results are uniquely evocative of motion and especially fascinating in colour.

Haas originally discovered the effect by accident. During the early fifties, he was photographing a bullfight in Spain and as the afternoon wore on, the action increasingly took place in the shadows. Since Kodachrome was so slow, he was forced into using shutter speeds as long as one-fifth or even one-half of a second. The blurred results intrigued him and he decided to experiment further (pages 14 and 15). In studying the pictures, he realized that the eye was always looking for some point of sharpness within the blur to hold on to. Ideally, he considered, that point should be the most important part of the image.

He found that the best way to achieve that effect was by 'panning' the camera, moving it in the same direction and relatively at the same speed as the principal subject, so that it stayed in approximately the same position in the viewfinder throughout the exposure. As a result, the background would be much more blurred than the subject, some parts of which would remain surprisingly sharp. Experience taught him how best to match shutter speed to the action.

Life published these bullfight photographs in July, 1957, under the title *Beauty in a Brutal Art,* and also commissioned Haas to apply the technique to various kinds of American sport. It was not a question of shooting to a proven formula. Each activity posed its own fresh challenge. Sometimes movements would be reasonably smooth and predictable, as in water-skiing. Sometimes they would be totally erratic, as in rodeo (pages 24 and 25). Haas is too adventurous in his approach to settle for easy options. As he has said, 'A formula is the death of everything. There always has to be some kind of a secret, some kind of a surprise. And the strange thing about aesthetics is that even if you do seem to have a formula, the very reverse is also true. For example, some people talk about colour formulas. that you should never use certain colours together and so on. But we can learn from painters that if there is such a colour formula, it can be broken. One can find a way to bring them together beautifully. If you arrive at a formula, try to go against it.'

The assignment went well and *Life* carried the pictures a year later as a two-part essay, *Motion in Sport.* Haas was also very articulate about the underlying philosophy of this work. 'The basic idea was to liberate myself from this old concept of a static moment and arrive at an image in which the spectator could feel the

continued on page 57

THE PHOTOGRAPHS

Venice, 1950s

Venice, 1950s

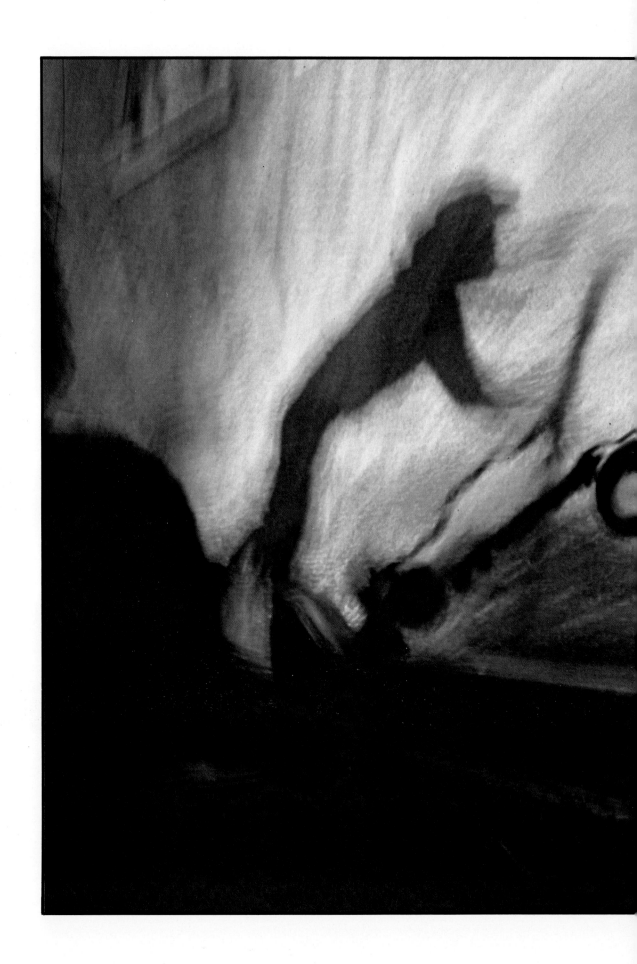

Venice, 1960

Venice, 1970s

Venice, 1975

Spain, 1970s

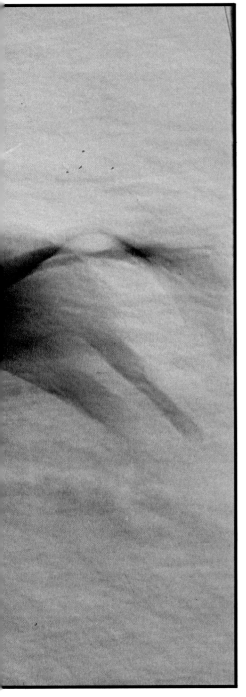

Spain, 1954   15

Spain, 1950s

France, 1950s

16

Chartres, France

London, 1960s

England, 1960

Racing on the beach, 1960s

Norway

Germany, 1970

Norway, 1960s

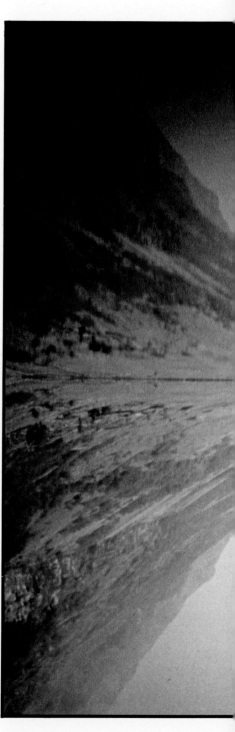

Norway, 1960s

Rodeo, 1970s

Rodeo, 1970s

Monument Valley, Utah/Arizona, 1967

Snow figures, from *The Creation*

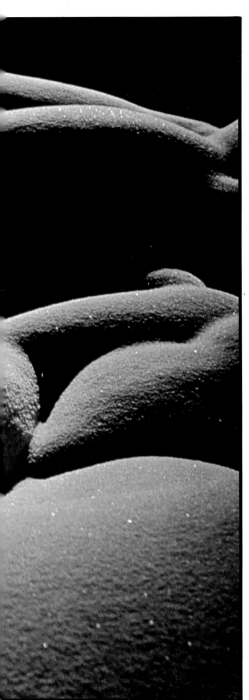

Wild horses, Nevada, 1960, from *The Creation*

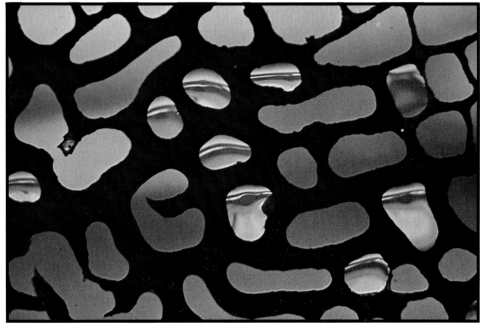

Water trapped in a coral, 1963, from *The Creation*

Space Museum, Florida, 1974

Gallup, New Mexico

Maine, 1975

The South West, USA

Reflected image, Chicago 1978

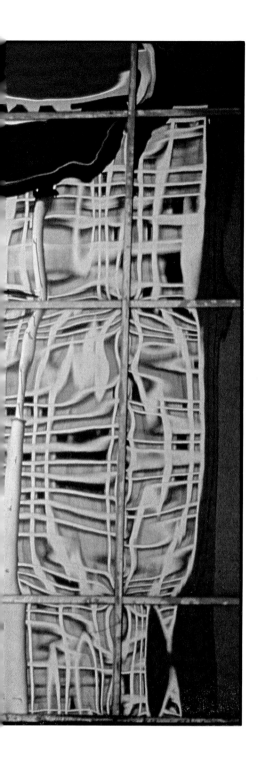

Pavement

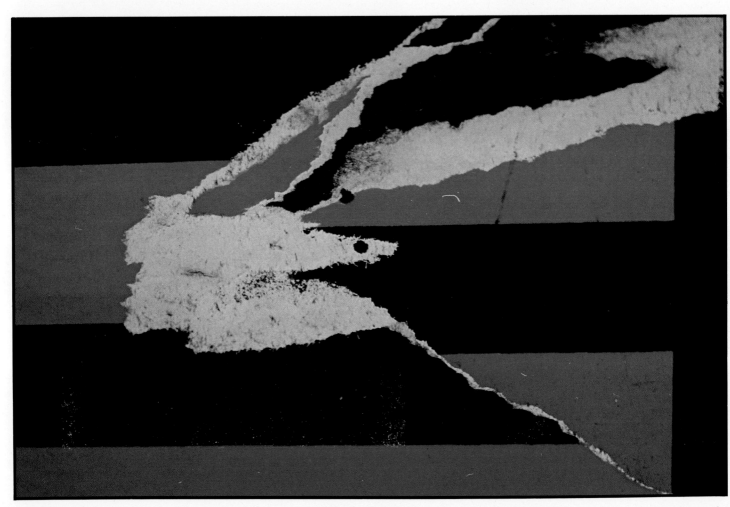

Poster, Los Angeles

Reflections, New York, 1960

Squashed clothing, New York, 1960s

Rooftop, New York, 1960

Central Park, New York

New York City

Rockefeller Plaza, New York, 1970s

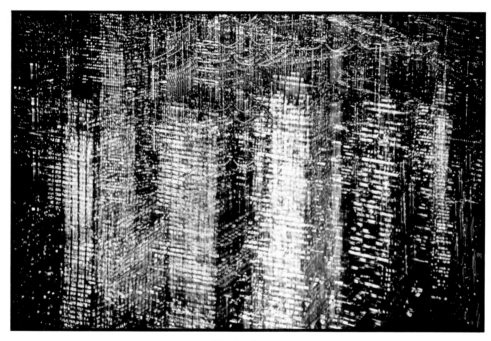

New York City

Mist, New York, 1980

The Brooklyn Bridge, New York

Lake Placid, New York, 1980

Hawaii, 1977

Colorado, 1978

Colorado, 1978

Colorado, 1978

Colorado, 1979

Colorado, 1979

Aspen, Colorado, 1981

Rain, Africa, 1970, from *The Creation*

Dharamsala, India, 1974

Pushkar, India, 1970s

India, 1970s

Bhutan, 1974

Japan, 1980

Japan, 1981

continued from page 6

beauty of a fourth dimension, which lies more between moments than within a moment. In music one remembers never one tone but a melody, a theme, a movement. In dance, never a moment but again the beauty of a movement in time and space.'

Curiously, one of his most striking photographs of movement was in fact of an absolutely motionless object (page 34). What appears at first glance to be a rather exotic bird in full flight was actually a fragment of a torn wall poster that he saw when he was walking through the streets of Los Angeles.

Haas has been quoted as saying, 'For me, the final stage of photography is transforming an object from what it is into what you want it to be.' Perhaps an even more surprising example of his talents in that direction is his picture of a piece of old clothing that has somehow been flattened out and squashed into the ground, possibly by a lorry (page 36). Not the most promising of raw material but Haas could recognize and reveal its astonishing icon-like quality. He has often shown a similar sensitivity to the forms, colours and patterns of apparently trivial urban details—a crumpled tin can, a paint scratch on a car, road markings (page 33), or an oil slick—handling them deftly with a light wit.

Once he captioned one of his photographs, 'The inanimate often suggests the animate'. It is a comment that could easily apply to several of these urban images, but he was actually writing about a landscape photograph (pages 28–29) where '. . . the smooth, flowing contours of newly fallen snow over stones in the bed of a shallow river bear an astonishing resemblance to human figures.'

This perceptive, sensuous and even amusing photograph appears in Haas's first book, *The Creation,* published in 1971, an imaginative tour-de-force interpreting the opening passages of Genesis in the Old Testament. The three chapters each represent one major theme: The Elements, The Seasons and The Creatures.

At the end of the book, he describes how the project gradually evolved. 'Perhaps the roots of it go back to the day I was born; certainly they lie in my early concern and fascination with natural history. But then, in 1959, I had an assignment with an industrial company which obliged me to think of dramatic ways in which to represent elemental power in photographic terms. I thought about the subject of power; I thought about the elements—air, water, fire, the earth. I also found myself thinking about sulphur, for, according to a text I had once read about alchemy, sulphur was once considered to be the fifth element. I went and viewed the sulphur pits in Yellowstone National Park, where the natural formations of sulphur reveal fantastic forms and textures. I took many photographs there, and in California; when the best of these were enlarged I found the results quite staggering. This led me to make further and further experiments along similar lines and in different regions of the world. It was not long before this new collection of photographs numbered in the thousands. I sorted them out and catalogued them in my library under such headings as 'air', 'fire', 'water', 'minerals', 'vegetation', ready for future use.

'At this time it so happened that I had an assistant by the name—believe it or not —of Michelangelo. And one day when I came back to the studio after a long assignment he had assembled a number of my photographs in the projector. With a sparkle in his eyes, Michelangelo turned on some music. It was Haydn's music. Then as he started to project the photographs, he said, "Do you realize what you have photographed? You have photographed the creation of the world." '

'Michelangelo said to me, "Do you realize what you have photographed? You have photographed the creation of the world." '

Haas then continued to refine the collection, add new photographs and finally edit the material into carefully blended sequences. The book was printed in Switzerland by C.J. Bucher Ltd with quite exemplary care and skill. The eventual result triumphantly vindicated, if any such justification was needed, John Szarkowski's judgement of almost a decade earlier. The creative range and consistent quality of the work live up to the ambitious nature of the undertaking. It is an exuberant, optimistic celebration of the world in which we live. (In autumn 1983, Viking Press of New York published a revised hardback edition of *The Creation* with about 40 new pictures.)

When Haas was asked a few years ago, what he looked for in photographing the landscape, he replied, 'I never really look for anything. A landscape for me is always a surprise because it depends on light. It depends on a certain relationship of colours and forms within space and then you have to figure out where do I put my frame, is it this area or that.

'That is one of the main differences between being a painter and being a photographer. The painter starts with an empty canvas and we always work on a full one.'

'That is one of the main differences between being a painter and being a photographer. The painter starts with an empty canvas and we always work on a full one. We have to place our frame so that we bring order to something which already exists. I would not call that a technique. Seeing goes together with thinking and feeling, and feeling is not a technique.'

When he was asked in a follow-up question whether he consciously tried to move the reality of a landscape into an abstract image, he answered, 'First of all, the abstract does not exist in photography. It is a word we borrowed from painting. If something we produce looks similar to an abstract painting, we call it abstract photography. But in fact it is a reality, it exists, and so the description is really false. We do not have a better name and so we apply it.'

The most abstract-seeming of Haas's pictures are usually those where the precise scale is uncertain—something small looks incredibly big, or vice versa. This play with dimension is very common throughout his work, sometimes consciously and sometimes instinctively produced. ('I have photographed for so long that it is almost like an experienced driver shifting gears. The more I photograph with pleasure, the less I think.') And so, for example, a section of a cave wall might be taken for a range of sand dunes or the reflection of sunset in an abalone shell could symbolize the very birth of the world. It reveals again how shapes and patterns interchange and echo throughout nature. Snow-covered rocks resemble nude figures, and a mosaic, possibly of lakes, ponds, puddles or pebbles, turns out to be the water-filled crevasses of coral, some droplets reflecting the beach, the sea and the sky (page 29).

Very occasionally, Haas has used special photographic effects to obtain unusual results. For instance, making a double exposure on the same frame of film, once in focus and then out of focus; sometimes even moving the camera position slightly between exposures. But however successful these experiments, he has no intention of becoming addicted to them. 'I do not want to be a super purist—no, on the contrary. But I have done it and there must be other ways of doing it. I do not need to re-do it again and again.' He is just as cheerful about using extreme focal length lenses very sparingly and for the most part, he relies on a very modest range of equipment. 'Of course today we are almost bored with normal things, so in order to get sensations we work with tricks. I wouldn't exactly say that a lens is a trick but if, for instance, you over-use a very wide-angle lens, you create a certain similarity of style and then the sensation that you want is lost through repeating it too often. Don't forget, there is one lens which we all forget—our feet. We can move closer or further away, which is generally very easy in the landscape.'

Now and again he has to depend on a technical ploy to solve a frequent natural problem, the very blueness of the sky. It can easily dominate a view, distracting attention from the patterns and subtler colours of land and water. Sometimes he simply composes the picture by cropping out the sky totally or partially. When that is not possible, he may use a polarizing filter to darken this penetrating, bright blue to a more bearable shade.

The landscape is widely represented too in his other books, often with animals, people, houses or other human artefacts giving a sense of scale and variety of interest. But his photograph of Monument Valley in the United States (pages 26 and 27) needed none of these extra elements. The first plate of *In America,* Haas said of it, 'I used this picture because I wanted to show the America which has been, is, and will be; that existed before we came and will survive after we are gone.' He took it from the air, braving the turbulent conditions in a small plane to catch the moment when the rain stopped, the clouds began to open and the sun shone through, giving strange light effects. The perfection of the composition under those circumstances is astounding.

'The frame of the camera is the photographer's discipline. It can contain as much as it withholds, cut into or hold together images that detract or contribute to a given theme.'

The scope of Haas's style can be seen if one compares this picture with all its richness of detail and colour, to a singularly spare image taken in Colorado in 1978 (page 47). One marvels that such specks of contrasting tone, the white cross and the moon, can assert themselves in so much space.

It is a classic example of his talent for simplicity, the ability to pare down to essentials. In the Introduction to *In America,* he wrote, 'The frame of the camera is the photographer's discipline. It can contain as much as it withholds, cut into or hold together images that detract or contribute to a given theme. Through it, lines, colors, form, and content all are seen to be related to each other in a very special way. Every nuance is important in heightening or weakening a composition.

'There are both a visual and a literal way of thinking and seeing. Over hundreds of years, the literal has dominated the visual until today our eyes are forced to see in terms of words. My plea is that as far as possible pictures should be allowed to speak their own language.'

That last paragraph also helps to explain why he decided against a movie-making career when he had the choice. He had been assigned to take special 'stills' pictures on movie sets since the mid-fifties, working on *The Pride and the Passion, Moby Dick, West Side Story* and *The Misfits.* Then in the sixties, he was employed as a second director on John Huston's film, *The Bible.* But he was not tempted to switch permanently from one medium to the other.

He realized that he would never enjoy the same freedom of expression in the movies as in 'still' photography and also that the priority of cinema was still largely narrative rather than visual. He is content in his chosen profession, in no way unsettled by the number of top photographers who seem anxious to move on to other art forms. But his life does not revolve exclusively around photography. His cultural interests are far wider, as is obvious from the way he lives, surrounded by books, paintings, tapestries, sculpture and other beautiful objects.

Haas made another important decision early in the sixties—he resigned from Magnum. The percentage of his income that went to the agency kept him constantly

Technical note

Haas's first professional photographs were taken with a Rolleiflex twin-lens reflex camera. However, he soon turned to using 35mm cameras and he has specialized in this format ever since.

An early devotee of Leica rangefinder models, he was quick to realize the advantages for his work of the newly-introduced single-lens reflex design. He has often stressed that, 'If I have any word of advice to give, it is that a photographer should learn to work with the minimum amount of equipment. The more you are able to forget your equipment, the more time you have to concentrate on the subject and the composition. The camera should become an extension of your eye, nothing else.'

Today he uses a very modest range of equipment for most of his work—two Leicaflex bodies and 35mm, 50mm, 90mm and 180mm lenses. He will however turn to other more extreme focal-length lenses if the situation really demands it. At one time he rarely carried a tripod but recently he has employed one more often.

The vast majority of his work is shot on Kodachrome 25 colour film but sometimes he has to use Kodachrome 64 because of its faster speed. Only in exceptional circumstances will he choose a much faster material, such as Ektachrome. He appreciates the superb resolution and middle-tone gradation of the slow emulsion.

in debt. His relationship with the organization was a friendly one and he was persuaded to give the arrangement one more chance. But it still did not work out and so he left. Over the years, he has tackled a broad variety, not only of editorial assignments but also of advertising commissions. There is nothing condescending in his attitude to commercial jobs and he finds considerable satisfaction in overcoming the technical problems that are often involved.

He also has the gift to discuss photography with a rare mixture of commonsense, perception and enthusiasm. As early as 1962 he wrote, directed and narrated four half-hour programmes on *The Art of Seeing* for American television, and then in the seventies he began to give teaching seminars. But much as he enjoys such activities, he firmly limits the amount of time he is prepared to devote to them. Otherwise the demand would soon eat into his normal work schedule.

In 1976, together with two other photographers, Jay Maisel and Pete Turner, he opened Space Gallery, to exhibit and sell colour prints. But though the market for black and white photographs was expanding rapidly, collectors were still wary of colour and so eventually the gallery closed down.

In recent years, Haas has become increasingly enthusiastic about more novel ways of displaying photographs—audio-visual shows. He enjoys exploring the more complex relationships between pictures that are possible in these presentations as compared to the printed page, and also the blending of images and sound.

Another fresh interest for Haas has been in Japan, a fascination that has probably developed from his earlier experience with the peoples of the Himalayas. He is intrigued by Asian philosophy and particularly now by the connections between nature and religion in Japanese culture. He visited Japan five times between 1981 and 1983, spending about seven months there in all.

Haas is very relaxed about the continuing controversy over the extent to which photography can be considered an art. He wrote, 'The pure definition of the word 'art' alone is today too vague for one to break one's brain and soul about it. Let us take a little vacation from this word. Let us work as well as we can, and it will come all by itself in which category we will be placed in the future . . . To compete with the painter is not really our destiny: we are on the way to speaking our very own language . . . Photography is in direct proportion with our time: multiple, faster, instant. Because it is so easy it will be more difficult . . . Everybody takes pictures, everybody can copy trends or styles . . . Only a vision—that is what one must have.'

This book began with a tribute to Ernst Haas by John Szarkowski and it ends with the words of his great predecessor, the late Edward Steichen, who said of Haas, 'In my estimation we have experienced an epoch in photography. He is a free spirit, untrammeled by tradition and theory, who has gone out and found beauty unparalleled in photography.'

Chronology

1921
Born in Vienna, Austria.

1947
First exhibition of his photographs, at U.S. Red Cross H.Q., Vienna.
Began working for *Heute,* an American magazine for Germans in the occupied territories.

1949
Heute and then *Life* published his memorable picture-story on returning prisoners-of-war.
Joined Magnum.

1951
Emigrated to the United States.

1960
First exhibition at Photokina, Cologne.

1961
Resigned from Magnum.

1962
Wrote, directed and narrated a series of four half-hour programmes for television, entitled *The Art of Seeing*.
Exhibition at Museum of Modern Art, New York.
Participated in and edited exhibition of *The world as seen by Magnum photographers* at Pepsi Cola Gallery, New York.

1964
Worked as a second director on John Huston's film, *The Bible*.
Exhibition at IBM Gallery, New York, of *Poetry in Color*.

1968
Exhibition at Asia House, New York, of *Angkor and Bali, Two Worlds*.

1971
Published his first book, *The Creation*.
Exhibition at Rizzoli Gallery, New York, of *The Creation*.

1972
Exhibition at Photokina, Cologne.
Selected for American Society of Magazine Photographers' Honor Roll.

1976
Opened Space Gallery, with photographers Jay Maisel and Pete Turner, to exhibit and sell colour prints.
Exhibition of *An American Experience* at International Center of Photography, New York.
Third exhibition at Photokina, Cologne.

Still based in New York City, Haas continues to travel widely on a variety of editorial and advertising assignments.

Bibliography

Books

The Creation, Viking Press, New York, 1971.
In America, Viking Press, New York, 1975.
In Germany, Viking Press, New York, 1976.
Himalayan Pilgrimage, Viking Press, New York, 1978.
The Creation (revised edition), Viking Press, New York, 1983.

Co-authored Books

Grand Canyon, Wilderness Series, Time-Life Books, New York, 1972/73.
Cactus Country, Wilderness Series, Time-Life Books, New York, 1973.
Venice, Great Cities Series, Time-Life Books, Amsterdam, 1976.

Movie 'Stills'

The Pride and the Passion, 1956.
Moby Dick, 1956.
West Side Story, 1960.
The Misfits, 1960.
The Bible, 1964.
Hello Dolly, 1968.
Little Big Man, 1969/70.
Electric Horseman, 1979.
Heaven's Gate, 1982.
Quest for Fire, 1982.

Selected Magazine Features

Heute, 3 August 1949, 'Returning Prisoners of War'.
Life, 8 August 1949, 'Returning Prisoners of War'.
Life, 15 September 1952, 'Land of Enchantment' (New Mexico).
Life, 14 and 21 September 1953, 'Images of a Magic City' (New York).
Life, 1 August 1955, 'Glow of Paris'.
Paris Match, October 1955, 'Asia-Africa Conference, Bandung'.
Holiday, February 1956, 'Oriental Utopia' (Angkor).
Life, 25 June 1956, 'Mirror of Venice'.
Holiday, August 1956, 'San Francisco Bay'.
Life, 29 July 1957, 'Beauty in a Brutal Art' (Bull-fighting).
Life, 11 and 18 August 1958, 'Motion in Sport'.
Esquire, August 1959, 'Bali'.
Holiday, January 1960, 'The Fjords of Norway'.
Holiday, July 1961, 'Magnificent West'.
Esquire, October 1962, 'Kick Off'.
Look, 21 May 1963, 'Spring Comes to England'.
Life, 1 November 1963, 'James Agee, Childhood Recreated'.
Sports Illustrated, 13 November 1967, 'France, A Go-Go Place for the Games'.
Geo, July 1979, 'Eighth Day'.
Life, November 1979, 'Cloud Land of the Spirits'.
Geo, April 1983, 'Bhutan'.

Index of photographs

First published in 1983 by
William Collins Sons & Co Ltd

London · Glasgow · Sydney
Auckland · Johannesburg

© 1982 Gruppo Editoriale Fabbri S.p.A.,
Milan

ISBN 0 00 411936 3

Typesetting by Chambers Wallace, London
Printed in Italy